From da Club 2 da Church House
Copyright © 2018, 2012 by Cynthia Young
Revised Edition

Printed in the U.S.A.

Published by Cynthia Young
First printed 2012

This book is based on real life events, however, some
names and identifying details have been changed to
protect the privacy of individuals.

Learn More www.glowyourgift.com

From da Club

2 da

Church House

Cynthia Young

Contents

Dedication

This book is dedicated to all those who inspired it. Those who were only with me for a season and those who are here for a lifetime. Oh, and I cannot forget about YOU! This one is for you too.

Introduction

I am back with a new revised edition to my original version of *"From da Club 2 da Church House"* which was originally published in 2012. For those of you who have read the original book, yes this is the continuation I promised I would write 5 years ago.

Most of the content in this version is the same as the original however I have added some new content as well as made some omissions. I have added one new chapter which is the final chapter of the book.

All original chapters remain and in the same order. This new chapter I believe sets the foundation for everything God is doing through me.

If you have not read the original version, don't fret because this new revised edition is not much different however I wanted to do a continuation from where I left off. What I have omitted is outdated information that no longer applies so if you have not read the original version, it's okay. This revised edition is sure to bless your life. What you will read next is the introduction to the original version of my debut book *"From da Club 2 da Church House"*.

From Monday night madness at Club Dreams to dollar shot Wednesdays at Sha-La, my face was one that was sure to be in the place week after week. I couldn't get off work quick enough to rush home and jump fresh to hit the club. There was one thing on my mind when I clocked out to go home, and that was party with a purpose.

My favorite club was the Sports Bar in Port Allen; a little hole in the wall right down the street from where I lived. My friends and I went there all the time. They played all the music I enjoyed listening to and all the hottest hits so it was the spot to be for the young adults.

Oftentimes, there would be a group of us when we hit the clubs, but sometimes I would roll solo.

Excitement filled our voices as we prepared to step into the party scene. We would always be at least 5 deep in there and looking like the divas we were when we walk in the club which meant all eyes were on us when we entered.

Now there were some other spots we would get off into. Bill's Place was right down the street. Just about everyone in there knew each other because most of the crowd was from Port Allen (PA) and there wasn't much drama like the clubs across the river.

Sipping on a long island iced tea or a long neck Budweiser in the middle of the dance floor was where you could find me. I loved to dance and still do love a good line dance every now and then. The words of Juvenile's back that thang up filled my ears and I was backing it up from the dance floor all the way to the center of the stage with my drink in one hand and my Kool filter king in the other.

At 2 o'clock am, most of the night clubs closed but the party didn't stop there because everyone just headed on down to Vibes 2.0 in Brusly, Louisiana. Vibes 2.0 closed at 4 am and it was the only club to stay open past 2:00 so for us who wanted to party a little while longer, we would just make our way over to Vibes 2.0.

Now this club attracted a large crowd from all the surrounding parishes and it's no secret the lines were always extremely long and it wasn't easy finding a good parking space. We would have to walk almost a half of mile to get to the door sometimes and on top of that, stand in a line wrapped around the building before getting in.

Imagine standing in line with 2 to 4 inch heels on and feet feeling like you've been walking through a field full of burning coals but that wasn't the case for me because I don't do stiletto heels and especially not in the club for that matter. The few times I called myself rocking stilettos in the club just wasn't a pretty sight if you know what I mean.

It went down at Vibes 2.0 every weekend and you were guaranteed to get kicked out the club before 4:00 because there would always be fights breaking out all over the club. All the DJ had to do is play a Lil Boosie track and the crowd went dumb, you know; retarded. Not to mention, we're already in there packed liked a can of sardines; dripping sweat, and soaking wet from our roller wrap on down to our toes.

Fights broke out every 15 minutes so if you're not in defense mode at all times, you could find yourself laid out on the floor in a heartbeat.

There is a patio on the outside where we could escape for a little relief but it would be in a moment's time when the patio was just as bad as the inside. The picture man out there was about 65 years old, but money is a motivator and despite all the drama, that didn't stop him from making his money.

All types of things occurred in there and nothing was off limits. Sexing, fighting, and drugs; you name it.

I had just made it through the door; paid my $20.00 cover charge and received my wrist band. Now it's time to enter the heat box. But moments later, the music is stopped and all I see is security dragging them clowns out the door by their collar because a fight has started.

Now the crowd is tagging along headed out the door and I'm forced to make a U-Turn and go right back out the door. The DJ is yelling in the mic "Get Out, Get Out, Party Over." Oh well there goes my hard earned $20.00 down the drain.

Now it's time to take it to the house and lay it down because I must be up and ready to go to church in a few hours. Oh yes that's right, I party on Saturday and be the first one up in the church house on Sunday. Don't act like you've never went to church with a hangover from the night before. Don't judge me!

Okay well maybe I'm the only one who was all up in the club on Saturday night and then found myself in the church house asking, "Lord please forgive me" on Sunday morning. I'll leave that alone! I know you don't behave like that; only me right.

The preacher would always deliver a word to convict me and have me feeling some type of way for partying half the night away but for me it was the same old sermon but a different Sunday. I had some nerve to be strutting my little behind in God's house after getting my drink on and shaking my tail all over the place a few hours before going to church.

Well we're all familiar with the saying "come as you are" so there I was as I was.

But today is a new day. My spirit is willing but my flesh is weak. I've already put it in my mind that I'm going to be the first one at the altar for altar call. Sure, I've had a desire before to go in front the congregation and publicly confess Jesus Christ as my Lord and Savior but Satan had other plans for me which was to keep me still in my seat. But, the devil is a liar today.

After the sermon was preached and Pastor extended me an invitation to Christian discipleship, I was the first one out of my seat and there was no turning back. This was the day! This was my season! I know many people associate their season with acquiring things and God opening doors but this was the most fruitful season of my life when I decided to live for Christ.

The Lord speaks to different people at different times and in different situations. He began speaking to me in the club which eventually led me to the Church House.

God spoke to me again and it was no different than any other time but this day for me was a new beginning. I couldn't run anymore. How could I, after all God had done for me?

Some may think I wasn't worthy and deserving of all God's promises but my Father assured me that I was worth more than silver and gold.

Therefore, if anyone is in Christ, he is a new creation; old things have passed away; behold, all things have become new... 2 Corinthians 5:17

1

To Every Thing

There is a Season

*G*rowing up as a child, I could remember attending service with my family and visiting with my friend's family at their church on occasion but I didn't go to church on a regular basis. Special times of the year such as Easter and Christmas was when I could remember always being at the church house.

Although, I was introduced to the Lord at a young age, I didn't understand who he really is or what that meant for me.

Sleeping during service is what my mind constantly reflects to as a child. However, Vacation Bible School was always fun and full of exciting activities. Vacation Bible School (VBS) was one of the church events I found to be of great interest to me.

So, I knew of this man called Jesus but to say I really had knowledge of his greatness would be an overstatement.

During my late teens, early twenties, I visited several churches in search of a church I could call home. I began to pray and ask God to place me in a loving and bible teaching church where I would be accepted and loved. I've had ministers and so-called prophets to lay hands on me and some thought they could predict my future.

I knew God was preparing me for what was to come. I know that some people claim to have this dramatic life changing experience which led them to follow the Lord but for me it was different. I felt I needed to search the scriptures for myself. I began to test the spirits because I knew all who claimed to be sent by God really wasn't.

I did acknowledge God but I didn't quite understand how much I needed him. My faith was small but according to scripture, little faith was all I needed. The Lord had been revealing to me through scripture that he had a plan for my life if I would just humble myself and submit to his will.

Thank God, he was patient with me and guess what, he's patient with all of us. I love the fact he will love us and bless us despite our faults. I would like to share with you some of my experiences and how I overcame many worldly desires of the flesh.

Ecclesiastes 3: 1 says, *to every thing there is a season, and a time to every purpose under the heaven.* That verse gives me great joy and hope in knowing that I have purpose here on earth and that I don't have to wait to transition to heaven before I can live out my purpose.

You see God has a purpose and a plan for each of us. What we are seeking is already in us, we just have to discover it for ourselves and tap into our greatness. We are all here for a reason and a for a season. We are not here by accident or coincidence but by divine appointment.

God knew you before you were formed in your mother's womb and he has a plan for your life. Is that great news or what?

And do not be conformed to this world, but be transformed by the renewing of your mind, that you may prove what is that good and acceptable and perfect will of God... Romans 12:2

2

No Discipline Seems Pleasant

at the Time

*A*t 15, most girls are thinking about clothes, boys, and parties. But Cynthia got pregnant -- and now she has to focus on raising her son. Everything changed for me in the summer of 1997, that is when I found out I was with child. I was 15 years young.

My pregnancy was considered high risk because I was only 15, but it turned out okay. Not to glorify having been pregnant as a teenager and especially out of wedlock, this was no glamorous situation but it was a learning experience for me and a turning point in my life.

My pregnancy lasted a little over 40 weeks and I thought my son would never make his entrance into the world. After hours of labor pain, I was finally given a cesarean section. I had become a mother to a precious baby boy and had not a clue in the world what was to come.

I've never been a typical teenager; I've always acted like I was older than I really was and I made it a point to hang out with the older crowd oftentimes. I've always thought outside the box and I have been strong when it came to my personality and who I am.

My parents were devastated when I first told them I was pregnant, but eventually they accepted the fact, they would soon be grandparents. Abortion & adoption just weren't options for me.

My family & friends all grew extremely supportive and I'm so thankful for them. My mother was reluctantly supportive; as she was trying to cope with her 15-year-old daughter who was to be having a baby and the reality of what that really meant to her.

Here I was 15, in love; (so what I thought anyway), doing well in school, and not a care in the world. I was also sexually active; and I had been since I was a freshman in high school. Transitioning over from middle school to high school was a different experience for me as I was beginning to discover who I was as a person and come in touch with my inner self.

Beauty became a top priority for me so I began to wear make-up and trying to dress to impress. Rocking the latest hair styles was a given because my big sister is a hair stylist so my hair stayed freshly done all the time. You couldn't tell me I wasn't grown and reality was I was living in an adult body with the mentality of an immature lost little child.

I didn't associate myself with child-like activities because truth be told, I thought I was grown and it wasn't long before I was doing things that grown folks do. I was out of control and off the chain!

After a few months into my pregnancy, I moved in with my boyfriend and his family. My father was angry with me for a while so I just distanced myself to avoid having to hear my father get on my case about my behavior. My father didn't like my boyfriend from the start because he felt Toby, who was my boyfriend and baby's father, wasn't any good for his baby girl.

Eventually, my father came around and he started to become excited that he would soon be a grandfather.

I continued to go to school and study hard throughout my pregnancy. In the beginning, it was a little embarrassing walking around school with my belly constantly growing but eventually I accepted my condition as a reality but not the norm. Everyone still treated me with the same respect so the only difference for me was that I had a life growing inside of me.

Around my fifth month of pregnancy, when my belly started to get a little bigger and my breasts started to get a little heavier, the father-to-be and I started to drift apart.

I don't think it hit either of us, until I started to show, how permanent this was. Once there was the "proof" that we would soon be parents, it dawned on him that soon he would be a dad and a parent with someone he didn't really know nor ever truly loved.

On a rush of hormones, adrenaline and fantasy, I still clung to the ever-persistent notion that it had to work. We had to be a family. We had created a life together, another human being, and that had to mean something.

By the time our child, a precious baby boy named Nijirren, had been born, things were seriously broken between his father and me. I was back and forth between living with him at his parent's house and with my parents. I was lucky to be able to continue high school, but like most young parents in my situation, I needed to seek government assistance to help with the insurmountable bills I never expected.

It wasn't long before I dropped out of high school at the end of my junior year and landed my first part-time job at Burger King. Toby couldn't keep a job and he just wasn't serious about his responsibilities as a father. Our parents had to help us take care of our son because our income just wasn't cutting it.

Reality came crashing down on me. I never had realized the demands and pressures that parenthood would bring. I was blessed to have supportive teachers, friends and family members, who, although sometimes overbearing, were always there for me. My son's father came by occasionally, and by the time I moved back home, he and I had become quite volatile toward one another.

We rarely spoke and when we did, it was never nice. He felt I had trapped him, and me still clinging to my childish fantasies, felt he had betrayed my love, and my trust. I laid a lot of the blame and guilt that I felt in his direction. It was much easier to feel less guilty myself by making him the bad guy.

When I turned 18, I moved out my parent's home and got myself an apartment. I allowed Toby to live with me because he confessed to me how sorry he was and that he wanted nothing more than for us to be a family again.

I was already aware of his unfaithful ways but I thought that things would eventually change for the better. Boy was I wrong! There had been several instances while we were together, when he had cheated on me. After he moved in with me, the cheating continued and things just went downhill all over again.

He still didn't have a stable job and I was working two jobs trying to make ends meet and take care of him at the same time. The bills started to become overwhelming and living on my own just wasn't all that exciting for me anymore especially since I didn't have any financial support.

After eight months of being broke, busted and disgusted, I moved back home with my parents because times were hard and money was tight.

Like many girls, I thought that if I had sex with a boy, it would mean that we were in love. I watched Toby feelings for me change just like I was afraid they would. I watched him cheat on me even though he said he still loved me.

Hurt feelings and a broken heart is what I recall time and time again because I trusted the words "I love you." It wasn't worth the pain or the drama!

Now when I reflect on my life in my teenage years and as a young mother, I can't help but give God glory from where he has carried me. The struggle was real and when I think of young mothers today having to raise children and many without a father around, my heart is saddened.

I was fortunate to have the love and support from family by my side because if it wasn't for them, I can't imagine where I would have ended up.

I want to encourage some young mother or even a mature mother who may be going through the motions of raising children all alone. Trust and believe God can and will carry you through whatever it is you may be experiencing in this season. You are not alone, God said he will be a mother to the motherless and a father to the fatherless. Just know whatever you need God to be, he can be that for you.

It was not easy raising a son as a young single mom with no real support from the father but God provided every need. It is hard enough raising children with two supporting parents so it is much harder as a single parent. Family planning and avoiding bringing children into the world before marriage I believe is the wise thing to do. Trust God; he will always provide!

Now no chastening seems to be joyful for the present, but painful; nevertheless, afterward it yields the peaceable fruit of righteousness to those who have been trained by it... Hebrews 12:11

3

He Must Manage
His Own Family Well

t all began in a sleepy little place called Port Allen, a small city down south in Louisiana. Louisiana is home of the mambo zydeco music and seafood & chicken gumbo. The red brick house on the corner as we would call it; is where I grew up. The family house was and still is a place I call home.

Three bedrooms, two full baths with a living and a dining area. No guest room or extraordinary outlet for entertainment, but it was a place of peace and a shelter of comfort.

Growing up as the middle child had its advantages as well as its disadvantages. My sisters and I got along with one another most of the time. If one of us did something we weren't supposed to do, we would stick together and have each other's back when it was time to suffer the consequences.

Since my big sister was much older than us, she didn't really share in the things my younger sister and I did as a child. My baby sister and I had many mutual friends so we did mostly everything together.

The kids in the neighborhood would always want to come over to my house because my mama was known for feeding a multitude which consisted of our friends from around the way. Everyone knew where they could get a good, hot meal. Mother loved to cook and she enjoyed feeding others. My mama's favorite dish to prepare was smothered pork chops w/ gravy and rice, cabbage and homemade cornbread.

Daddy went to work every day; Monday through Friday from 4:30 in the morning until 5:00 in the evening. He worked as a janitor at Trinity Marine; a barge manufacturing company, in a small town called Brusly about ten miles from where we lived.

He had the privilege to drive the company truck to run errands oftentimes while at work. He was a faithful and loyal employee with over 30 years of service. We could expect my daddy home around lunch time every day on his lunch break, and no doubt mama would have a hot meal waiting for him when he arrived.

My parents were in love and it showed through their actions. My mama never had to work outside of the home because my daddy always provided for his family. We had one family car, a small red two doors 1979 Datson 210 back in the day which transported us wherever we needed to go.

Some mornings my mama would have to wake us up at 4:00 in the morning to take my daddy to work. On the days, my mama would keep the car, we would go to the Ferry and visit with my grandmother and sometimes visit with other relatives.

My mama loved traveling and wherever she went, we were always one step behind her.

{Grandma's House}

Grandma is what we called my grandmother Emma. She was the sweetest little lady and so full of joy. I still have memories of her sitting in her favorite chair in the corner of her bedroom smoking on her pipe stuffed with Kite tobacco. Her grandkids brought a lot of joy to her life and we made her day just by being in her presence.

She always talked to us about God and taught us a lot about the bible and how to treat others. A lot of my time was spent in the Ferry at grandma house when I was a child. Now, grandma house was the spot to be on the regular because of all the fun we had there.

Everyone in the neighborhood liked to hang out there from my uncle's friends on down to our friends. On holidays, the whole family would gather at grandma house for great food and entertainment. That big homemade pot of beef vegetable soup was her signature dish and was sure to have us licking our fingers down to the last scoop.

Now there is Jr.; that is what my grandma called him. Jr. is my mama's only brother and considered to be the baby although he isn't the youngest of my mama's six siblings.

He lived at home with my grandparents for as long as I could remember. Uncle June had a way of getting whatever he wanted out my grandparents. He is that family member who always has a drink in his hand but we all love him to life.

Grandma would call the police on him and have him removed from the home when he would get drunk and start acting a fool and then be waiting at the jail to bail him out before he could be processed and booked.

She'll make it to the jail before the police got there with him. Now that is a trip.

Grandpa was cool and laid back most of the time. He had retired from the State Times, so he just occupied his time by keeping his grandkids happy.

He had this old shed on the side of the house where he stored all types of tools, old equipment, bicycle frames, and other stuff. He would sit in the front yard and piece together bicycles for the children who lived in the neighborhood. One thing we all had was a bicycle to ride, thanks to my grandpa.

It was no secret that sometimes we had a 12-speed frame with 10 speed wheels, six different colors, or that the handle bars were taken from a tricycle; we were rolling and that's all that mattered. I still break out in laughter when I think about the bicycles my grandpa used to put together for us.

But the bikes had nothing on the wooden swing grandpa tied to the tree in the front yard with a rope that held approximately 4 people at a time.

Now you know we were 10 deep in that swing every time it went into the air. Yeah, there were many days we were picking each other up off the ground dusting one another off after the swing parted ways with the tree (lol). That was some good throwback fun and we were busted and scratched up many of days.

{Sandy}

We called my mother Sandy instead of calling her mama. It was a substitute for Sandra. My mother was the kindest person I have ever known and she always kept a smile on her face that would light up a dark room.

Everywhere she went, she would initiate conversation with complete strangers about any and everything. All my memories of her consist of being kind to her family and others.

Sandy was very beautiful; dark complexion, brown eyes, long cold black hair, and about 5"4 tall. She loved to visit with family and friends on a regular to pass time. It didn't matter what time of day it was, she would show up at your house unannounced and expect you to be welcoming with open arms.

That was cool of course because everyone knew how she was so they just accepted it. Family ties back in those days is what kept us going.

My mama always liked traveling and she would take a trip in a heartbeat with no planning involved.

For instance, there was a time when we ended up in San Francisco, California after driving for three days in a Datson 210 with little to no money. Our journey began one evening after Sandy asked my daddy to borrow the car to run to the supermarket to pick up some groceries. But, that is not exactly how it all happened; she had plans far beyond taking a trip to the store.

Me and my baby sister Danielle tagged along on this journey in which we thought we were just making a run to the store. Now after riding for a few hours, I began to wonder where in the world we were going.

But, before I could ask the question, she told us that we were going to visit with a cousin in California and it would take us about three days to get there. Okay mind you, we only had a few dollars and a ¼ tank of gas.

We stopped a few times to gas up but sooner than later, we were all out of money. Now we weren't even half way to our destination and already out of funds.

My mother, being the person, she is, not afraid to converse with strangers, asked someone at the gas station for money to buy food to eat. The Good Samaritan gave my mother some funds to help us on our journey. I guess we were what you would call a panhandler today but we made it safe and sound. I still don't know how we made it or exactly how much money my mama was able to pull off but we made it to Cali eventually.

God always provides a way! Thinking back on the many trips I took as child, this is one that has stuck with me and I remember it like it was yesterday because I know God was with us every step of the way. Not to mention, my mother wasn't all the way in her right mind.

She knew we had a relative that lived in San Francisco but wasn't sure of the exact location. This was just one of the many spur of the moment trips we journeyed along on with my mother.

Once we arrived in San Diego, we checked into a shelter where we stayed for a short period until we were rudely kicked out because my sister had been crying out of control throughout the night. We finally could find out where my cousin lived so we made our way over to my cousin's house the following day.

By this time, my daddy and everyone is worried sick about us back home in Louisiana because nobody knows where we are or if we are okay or not. My daddy filed a missing person report because he didn't know where in the world we could be.

No one had heard from us or seen us in three days. So, to make a long story short, my daddy finally located us and brought us back to Louisiana. In California is where I had my first experience of an earthquake.

Right before we were getting ready to check out the hotel we were staying in, an earthquake hit and kept us in California a little while longer. It was such a horrifying experience and my mama promised to never skip state with us again under those circumstances.

My mother was diagnosed with a mental illness at an early age which she depended on medication and treatments throughout her entire adult life. Many people never knew about my mother's illness because as long as she continued her treatments, she was okay.

There were times when she just didn't want to continue her meds so she would miss her doctor's appointments and stop her meds. We always knew when this happened because she would behave differently.

She would begin to hear voices and become irritable & aggressive. We've had to commit her to several mental institutions when things really got bad but it was only for short periods because she couldn't stand being away from us for too long.

Despite her mental illness, she was still the sweetest and kindest person you could ever want to meet. Sandy loved us and cared for us dearly, and that is what I miss the most about my mother. When I think back on all the memories of my mother, I could just see those same characteristics in myself now that I'm an adult. People who knew my mother always tell me I'm the spitting image of her.

{Teddy}

Ted or Lil Ed is what most people call my father but for my sisters and me, we call him Teddy. My daddy is the hardest working man I've ever known and he taught us what it means to be responsible. He worked very hard every day to provide us with the things we needed.

His work didn't end when he made it home in the evening after working 12-hour shifts either. He always found something around the house to get into. We admired my father for his continued efforts to keep us happy.

My father loved all types of entertainment and his passion was his music. He is an artist and could play several different instruments. Teddy and some of his friends formed a blues band when I was young. My daddy was the lead singer and he played the drums and guitar too.

They would get together every weekend and play music underneath the car port which attracted many visitors to our house.

Sandy and her friends would be cheering them on, sipping on their miller lite and you couldn't tell them they weren't at a blues concert (lol) There were always so many kids at our house so we had so much fun too, singing and playing the drums.

Our house was the spot to be although we had some neighbors who would from time to time call the police and report that we were disturbing the peace because the music was so loud. Now that I think back on those Friday evenings when we had the block lit every single weekend, I would have called the Police too.

The beat of 'I'm a soul man" would be blasting from the woofers. The entertainment lasted for a while until my daddy just started doing his own thing but he never gave up his music. He still sits in the living room from time to time with his karaoke machine singing his heart out.

My daddy enjoyed amusements parks and festivals; in fact, we were always on a mission whether it be to a blues festival in downtown Baton Rouge or to Fun Fair Park also located in Baton Rouge. There wasn't much to do in Port Allen so for entertainment we had to go to the east side. He challenged us all the time to get on some of the scariest roller coaster rides with him.

Every summer my father took us on a family vacation. Astro World in Houston, Texas was our signature spot for a long time and the three times we visited Disney in Orlando, Florida was an experience of a lifetime. We had so much fun and my daddy acted as if he was a kid again when it came to thrills and rides.

Those memories of our time spent together having fun as a family hold a special place in my heart and in my mind.

In 1992 my parents agreed to sign a document of divorcement but funny thing is, they never divorced each other. My parents never really separated and we all still shared the same home.

It was evident to me they didn't desire to be married any longer but they still loved one another. My father continued to work hard and provide for us. Although my parents were legally divorced, they felt it was important to keep us together as a family.

Love to the highest degree was displayed in our home and I'm thankful for parents who acknowledged the possibilities of what could have happened had our family separated because of a divorce decree. So, I'm convinced that anything is possible when love is in the equation.

It was just me and my two sisters for a long time until my baby brother was born. He is the youngest of my father's 5 children. I also discovered some years later that I had another brother.

Now that my mom and my two brothers mother are deceased, my dad is now left to hold the family down. For holidays and birthdays, he would always have a full course meal cooked for us. He loves to cook for us and I'm so grateful.

My niece Diamond keeps him on his toes and he's right there supporting her for every dance practice and recital and the tons of other extracurricular activities she's involved with.

For better or for worse is what comes to mind when I think of my parents' undying love for each other because my father was there for my mother when she became terminally ill and he was right there by her side when she took her last breath.

For you, O Lord, are good and forgiving, abounding in steadfast love to all who call upon you... Psalm 86:5

4

In All Toil
There Is a Profit

I've always been a hard worker and it doesn't matter what my job duties consists of, I strive to be the best I can be. It doesn't matter if I'm flipping burgers or scrubbing toilet seats, I take great pride in my work. My work history began at the young age of 12 as a shampoo technician for my big sister Bridget.

Every weekend, I was in the hair shop from 6 am until whatever time we finished with the last walk in client. Instead of me watching my favorite cartoons on a Saturday morning, I was massaging scalps and practicing good housekeeping skills in the beauty shop.

I worked in fast food and customer service mostly during my first years in the workforce. I held my first supervisor's position when I worked at Arbys at the age of eighteen. At first, I didn't want to accept the position because of all the responsibility that came along with the job, but eventually I accepted the offer.

I had already witnessed the issues the other supervisors were dealing with such as employees not showing up for work and when they do decide to show up, they do a poor job. So, I pretty much already knew I was in for a challenge which is why I really didn't want the position in the first place. At that time, I had just moved out my parent's house and was living on my own.

I was one of the youngest employees working there at the time and I found it hard to believe they chose me as a candidate for leadership. But I guess I was the best fit for the job. Well, after a few talks with my mama about how I can use the extra money to cover bills was what motivated me to take the job.

Arbys stayed open 24/7 which meant we operated on three shifts which included the dog shift nobody wanted to work. There were a lot of times when I would have to work double shifts to cover for the ones that didn't show up for work.

My regular shift was 3-11 in the evening but I would have to stay over and work 11-7 overnight too for others who would not show up for work. Some nights the store ran itself because I was just too darn tired to be bothered.

This one particular night after I had all I could take and I just couldn't do it any longer; I locked up the store and went home around 3 am. I quit! Oh yes, I surely did! Well that was my last night working as an employee for Arbys. That wasn't the first job I had quit and it sure wasn't to be the last. After leaving that job, I was hired at Shoney's where I worked as a server and bar attendant for a few months.

And after I left Shoney's, I started working at Waffle House. Waffle House was different from any other fast food job I had and it took me a minute to learn the system and become an effective waitress. The whole idea of calling in orders on the mark was new for me.

I sure messed up a lot of orders and not to mention, I was bringing the wrong food to the wrong tables at times. But eventually after a few months of practice and experience, I was calling in those order scrambles and hash browns smothered, covered, chunked, diced and topped with confidence.

I was doing my thing and I was getting big tips, especially from the drunkards on the weekend. I enjoyed my job and I was very thankful to have income coming in but there was still so much missing from my life and I was eager to start searching for the missing pieces to the puzzle.

{*Evil Matrimony*}

Before the date was set and final, I already knew I was making a huge mistake by planning to marry Toby. Although, a lot of people I knew were getting married for all the wrong reasons, I wanted to share a special bond with my husband that no man could separate, kind of like the bond I now have with God.

Me and Toby had been together on again and off again for 10 years before we were married. Marriage was something we had talked about over the years but never really put much thought into it.

But it wasn't until after Toby had just finished serving a 2½ year prison sentence, is when I decided to make it official. You see I said I decided to make it official and not us make it official. My first mistake.

In my mind, I thought Toby was ready for a change. I believed this last prison bid had redeemed him and changed him into the man God required him to be and the man I needed him to be. So, the date was set March 25th, 2005, which was two months after his release.

I handled all the planning, coordinating, and decorating for my wedding. We were on a tight budget so funds were limited for the occasion but I managed everything well. The two months prior to my wedding, I spent most of my time planning and researching.

During this period, things began to take a turn for the worst not to mention all the other drama. We attended a few marriage counseling sessions prior to the wedding but all we did was put on a front as though everything was all good when in reality it really wasn't.

We went at each other throats all night long the night before the wedding. So many different emotions were displayed that night. I cried so much the night before my wedding; I just wanted to call the entire thing off. But instead, I pressed my way to the beauty shop at 6 am to get all dolled up for my big day.

I did manage to get about two hours of sleep so I was able to hide the hurt and the bags around my eyes from the night before.

The wedding took place at my parent's home and everything turned out beautiful. I don't think anyone suspected how bad things were and that I was an emotional wreck inside. Deep down inside I knew I was making a huge mistake by marrying Toby, but after I said those vows followed by an "I Do", it was no turning back.

After Toby and I left the club on our wedding night, the most memorable thing happened after we were pulled over by the police. Toby had been driving and of course he had had his share of crown on the rocks that evening. We pulled over on side of the road and as the officer was approaching our vehicle, Toby hopped out the car and took off running through the yard of the house which we were stopped in front of.

I'm looking like; I know this clown didn't just jump out this car and flee in that tuxedo looking like the Joker at a marathon. The cops didn't even chase him; they were laughing so hard, it was unreal. They even videoed the entire thing and recommended the clip for America's funniest home videos.

If that wasn't enough for one day, I don't know what was. I thought the day couldn't get any worse. Well I was wrong.

We were finally on our way home and as we were approaching the stop light to turn two blocks from the street I lived on, our car just stops in the middle of the intersection. The battery checked out and died in the car. So here we are on Florida Blvd. at Three in the morning pushing the car in wedding attire and sweating like Hebrew slaves.

Talk about a wedding day nightmare. But at the end of the day, we were still husband and wife.

Well it shouldn't come as surprise that this union only lasted six months before I was filing for legal separation. In the between time, the abuse didn't end. We continued to go at each other throats constantly and the cheating just made things worst.

My grandmother passed away a few months later and instead of Toby being there to comfort me through this trying time, he was laid up with another woman that lived directly across the street from where we shared a home. I would literally stand and look out my bedroom window and see them coming and going together while I was at home praying to God for my marriage and restoration.

The more I cried and prayed, seem like the farther apart we became. I had cried my last tear over Toby and I had made up my mind that enough was enough. My first marriage was very short lived; 6 months to be exact before we separated for good. The pain and shame of living separated was a lot to handle but with God's strength, my faith was renewed every day and it was not long before I realized God was keeping me even through the mess.

Although I was hurt I was confused I was angry and I was ashamed; it wasn't hard for me to forgive. I never wished any evil on anyone and I didn't seek to get revenge. I just remember praying to God to get me through because I believed God would deal with those who wronged me and I still believe that to be true today. God was fighting my battles for me even when I didn't know it. Pray for those who wrong you. Forgiveness is for your peace not the person that tried to break you.

I never found blame on those women who my husband cheated with because I didn't make a vow to them. I respected them even though I was disrespected and I'm sure some knew of our relationship but it didn't matter to them. I have been the other woman myself so I knew how to play the game.

That failed relationship was actually working for my good. My failed relationships were successful, I just didn't know it in that season. My failed relationships helped to prepare me for my destiny and the wife I believe God needs me to be.

Ten years later I met my husband Andre who I have been married to now for three years. He is my rock and I couldn't have asked for a better person that brings out the best in me yet challenges me to take a look in the mirror when I'm not at my best.

You couldn't have told me back then when I was in that dark place in my life that God had a divine plan for me and if I would just surrender all, God would do a work in me when the time was right.

When we are in our storm, we can't see what is on the other side but if we would surrender and trust God, he can reveal to us his divine plan when the time is right.

If God would have given me what I was praying for in that season, I wouldn't have been able to handle it at that time. God has to withhold some things from us until we are mature and ready to receive it. Every good and perfect gift comes from above. When I began to truly understand this, my life began to shift.

No longer did I receive everything that was negatively affecting me as a curse but some experiences were a blessing in disguise and without those obstacles and bumps in the road, I don't know if my skin would be thick as it is now.

It was painful but it was indeed necessary. Necessary to get me closer to the promise.

{Falling in Love with Yourself}

A strong relationship with oneself is a necessary precursor to every other relationship in life. If you don't have a solid relationship with yourself, you will recklessly pursue external relationships and you will try to love others in a desperate need to find in them what you must find within yourself.

You will do the right things for wrong reasons and grapple disappointment that comes from expecting someone to give you what you must give yourself.

While people will change and you will change, it is nice to be fastened to something that is always the same. Anchor yourself in the Lord. Who can restore what life has taken out of you, but God?

{Kool Addict}

Kool was my brand of choice for cigarettes. I took my first puff on a cigarette when I was 14 years old. My mother smoked regularly so when she would leave one lit in the ashtray on the table, that was my opportunity to sneak a puff while she was in another room.

I had no idea at the time; it would lead to a long exhausting fifteen year addiction to nicotine. I knew other kids my age who were smoking so I wanted to experiment and try smoking too. It wasn't long before I would have to get older people to purchase cigarettes for me because I wasn't of legal age to buy them myself.

After smoking for over a decade, my desire to quit was stronger than my desire to continue. I knew the effects of smoking and I didn't want to be another statistic. Cynthia dead at 30 the news headline would read. The devil is a liar.

I began to take steps to kick the habit but after a few failed attempts, I just say to hell with it because the urge to smoke was so strong. Some of my friends smoked and a lot of the people I worked with smoked cigarettes so even when I would go on my two or three-day non-smoking episodes, I would quickly fall back into the trap.

I just began to accept smoking as a way of life for me because it was too hard to quit and I began to think I didn't stand a chance. People would constantly say to me all the time when they see me smoking that I don't look like I smoke.

Well, I often wondered what a smoker looks like because obviously I sure didn't fit the description according to others.

Comments like those were my motivation to kick the habit once and for all. I was smoking a pack or more a day sometimes.

In 2006, my mother was diagnosed with throat cancer, and I'm sure her excessive smoking was a huge contributing factor to her illness. The cancer really took a toll on my mother and it was so painful to experience her suffering.

After undergoing chemotherapy and radiation repeatedly, she became weary. We were soon faced with the unimaginable. The doctor told my mother she had a few more months to live.

I had never heard of hospice and I didn't know exactly what their role was and what that meant for my mother. The doctor sent us on our way and informed us that we would now be in the hands of hospice care and there really wasn't much more they could do.

By this time, my mother could not eat any solid foods and it hurt me so deeply to watch her hunger around the clock. Her diet consisted of liquids only and her weight was at an all-time low.

She was miserable and it wasn't anything I could do but feed her morphine day in and day out to ease the pain. The hospice team was very helpful and we were so very grateful for them because without them, I don't know how we were going to continue to watch my mother die a slow and painful death.

But through all of that, she still smoked every now and then when she had the strength to. She had been smoking nearly two packs of cigarettes a day for as long as I can remember, so a cancer diagnosis sure wasn't about to stop her now. Now when I see people pulling their breathing machine with one hand and taking a puff off a cigarette in the other, I'm deeply saddened because I myself watched my mother do the same thing during her last days. I vowed to never put myself in that same situation under those circumstances.

It was the early morning of February 24th, 2007 when my mother was called home to glory. She had smoked her last GPC full flavor 100 and taken her last breath. On that day, a part of me left with her. Before my mother became very ill to the point where I was there with her all the time, she was the type of mother that called every day and sometimes several times a day just to hear my voice.

We prayed & cried, cried & prayed, and did all we could do to keep her here with us a little while longer but God was ready for Sandy to go home.

Well I sure wish I could say, that was the last time I lit up a Kool filter king but I can't. I so badly wanted to just quit cold turkey and never look back after what I had seen my mother go through. I knew deep down I had to quit or I would eventually experience the pain my mother felt.

After my mother died, I attempted several times again to quit because I was just in so much pain from my mother's death and I didn't want my child to experience what I went through with my mother. I tried all types of quit smoking aides. It was with the Nicoderm CQ patch I had my greatest success but it was only for a moment before I was swooped back into the trap before quitting cold turkey. For anyone who smokes or smoked in the past, I know you can attest to the struggle I was caught up in.

In the meantime, during my failed attempts to quit, I began smoking black & Mild as a substitute but I only went from bad to worst. Eventually I became addicted to cigars. It was a no-win situation for me.

I became exhausted from having such a strong desire to quit but not able to pull through. I then resorted to the electronic cigarette as a means of quitting but that didn't help either. I needed God's help and that was the only way I knew I was going to get through this thing.

"Lord release this stronghold" was my continued prayer. I knew my body was a temple and

I wasn't supposed to be polluting my body with all those toxins but I had been smoking for a long time and it had become a part of my world.

Through prayer and meditation, I was finally able to gain control of my life. During this time is when I first began my journey of fasting and prayer. I will talk more about my spiritual journey later in the next few chapters.

I encourage anyone who has struggled with nicotine addiction or any other addiction, to never give up trying. I can assure you that anyone who has ever tried to break any addiction were not very successful their first few attempts. Whether it is crack cocaine or crown black on the rocks, it's a challenge overcoming addiction to any chemical dependency.

It's not worth it one way or another. It takes a lot of strength and courage to break those kinds of addictions. My journey to nicotine recovery has been long and challenging but I made it. What a wonderful feeling! It has been 7 years now since I smoked my last Kool Filter King and I can assure you if I was able to kick the habit, you can too.

Sharing this may not touch you personally or affect you in any way but for a smoker or an ex-smoker knows exactly what I went through. I know a lot of people who still struggle with this and it's a uphill battle for someone who desire to take control of their life in this area so I know somebody needs to hear this.

It took me doing a lot of studying and research to educate myself about nicotine addiction. Much prayer and fasting. I didn't attend any smoking cessation programs or solicit the help from anyone other than God. God gets all the glory!

I had to learn that the same people who were producing and selling the cigarettes are the same ones who turn around selling the stop smoking aids; the patch, electronic cigarettes, gum, etc. Either way it goes, they are profiting off your destruction. The enemy is out to destroy us and he succeeds by keeping us bound by the things that bring us the most painful pleasure.

I want to watch my grandkids kids grow up and my mother could not experience that. She died when her only two grandchildren were 10 years and 6 months old.

{Applied Knowledge is Power}

I always knew I would eventually go back to school and get my high school diploma someday. I really liked school and I wish I would have finished and graduated considering I only had one year left before I dropped out.

Continuing my education was something I always thought about but I just did not find the time or get around to pursuing my educational goals.

I knew I had to learn some type of skill and further my education if I ever wanted to bring home anything more than minimum wage.

When I was a kid growing up, I always said I would be a teacher one day. I just wanted to be a leader and help others in some way.

It was fall of 2007 when I really made up my mind to take the GED test. On the day of testing, I was very excited and proud of myself for taking that first step. I was confident I would pass with flying colors. After several hours of testing, I was exhausted from thinking so hard and I was hungry. Once I completed my testing, I would have to wait several weeks for the results to arrive in the mail.

The day was December 29th, one day before my 26th birthday, when the results from my GED arrived in the mail. I was full of excitement when I learned I had mastered all parts of the test. After years of procrastination, I had finally earned my high school masterpiece and I was elated.

My two sisters were a strong motivating factor for me. They both constantly tried encouraging me to go back to school and I would continue to make excuse after excuse. They never lost hope in me despite what I had been through and I thank them so much for their continued love and support.

I had been employed at Ryan's Steakhouse for the past three years as a mega bar cook. This was the longest I had ever been on a job and I felt I had accomplished something for once in my life. Ryan's wasn't the best job in the world but it kept food on the table and gas in my bucket that got me from point A to point B every day.

The turnover rate was extremely high and I had seen over a hundred-people come and go during the few years I was there. I was constantly training new people every other week but training pay for me wasn't even an option.

We were like family at Ryan's and I loved the people I worked with. My hours were long and tiresome oftentimes. Sundays were our busiest work day of the week. Business was usually booming on Sundays because people came to eat after church service. The store would be packed to capacity.

I couldn't get the food on the buffet quick enough for some of the guests behaving like untamed wilder beasts on the prowl for food. That buffet was a hot mess when they finished tearing it up. The wait staff got their dollars up on Sundays and so did I because while I was waiting for food to finish cooking in the kitchen, I'll go on the floor and catch the tables that were neglected by their waitress. Those days were all grind for me and no play.

I had become a valued employee to the company but little did they know, I had bigger and better plans and I would soon be saying goodbye.

After I obtained my GED, I began researching colleges because I wanted to continue my education. I had dreams of going back to school to pursue several career paths but Criminal Justice was a field I had always been thinking about a lot.

As I grew older, I didn't watch much television but when I did decide to watch T.V, I was fascinated by court TV and law & order. I loved me some Judge Mathis and People's Court. I don't turn on my T.V much these days so I can't say much about the latest court shows or anything else that is on the airways for that matter.

I don't even want to get into all the foolishness that is on T.V now. In my humble opinion, people spend way too much time watching T.V and not enough time reading.

So, I couldn't afford to attend a big university with my current salary so my options were limited to the local community colleges. But that was cool with me because I was just excited to finally be able to pursue some of my goals I've had set but never really had that right opportunity. I had contacted several schools before I made my decision to enroll at Remington College. My recruiter was very helpful and she seemed really concerned about me continuing my education.

The enrollment process by itself gave me butterflies because after ten years, I was going to soon be back inside of a classroom. I was immediately invited to the school for a tour and we got the ball rolling from that point on. I was accepted and two weeks following my enrollment, I was officially a student studying in the field of Criminal Justice (CJ). I went to school 3 nights a week and worked during the day.

My supervisor wasn't too pleased when I began attending school because that meant I couldn't continue to work all those long and crazy hours anymore.

I had given them a notice in advance that I would be starting school and that some adjustments would need to be made to my schedule. My boss wasn't trying to hear that. He continued to schedule me to work hours that were conflicting with my school schedule so it wasn't long after that I resigned from Ryan's.

I always envisioned what it would be like to be a college student considering I was a high school dropout. Education wasn't at the top of my priorities before. I just didn't have time for school, I had to work and make sure the bills were paid and food was on the table.

I really enjoyed going to school unlike some of my other classmates who constantly complained about how hard it was to work and attend school. It definitely was a challenge for me don't get me wrong but I made the sacrifice each and every day to get up, show up and do what I needed to do.

While in college, I learned that school isn't difficult at all or anything for that matter, if you just apply yourself and study diligently. I used to believe that when I failed in grade school, it was because the teachers just didn't want to teach me or the work was too hard.

Well as I look back now, I realize I just wasn't applying myself and reaching my full potential. I maintained a 3.5 Grade Point Average (GPA) or above and I was on the president's list numerous times which meant I had a 4.0 GPA that quarter. My instructors were very knowledgeable about the CJ field and I learned a wealth of knowledge to prepare me for the work force.

One of my instructors, Ms. Tiffany, is someone I admire dearly and I would never forget her continued effort to make sure her students achieve their best and accomplish the goals we had set.

She made it a point to make sure we were in class every day and if we weren't there by a certain time, she would give us a friendly reminder call or text to confirm we were on our way to class. She is the greatest and you don't find too many like her around anymore. She wanted to make sure we were getting every penny worth of education we paid for.

Everything she did for us was out of love and concern and we acknowledged her efforts.

I graduated with honors in the spring of 2010 and the joy I felt was too big for words to explain. Those two years had been a challenge for me but I pressed my way through it just like I knew God would give me the strength to. I encourage anyone who has been placing their dreams and goals on the back burner to go forth with it.

It is never too late to achieve the goals you have set in your heart. You must realize that you are ultimately responsible for the outcome of your life. If you don't know something, find out. If you are lacking a skill, learn it.

A world of information is available to you if only you have the desire to improve your condition. It's about recognizing possibilities and working hard to take full advantage of them.

Society and prosperity are about results. What value you bring. The reality is no one cares why you are late, why you make bad grades, why your dad left, why your mom couldn't afford new clothes for you, or why your heat wasn't on every winter and you had to use the stove for warmth. The real world is about showing up and producing.

College teaches us a lot of things, little of which is taught in the classroom. We learn important lessons about love, life, sex, and of course, money.

Many of us aren't quite sure what we want to do and there's nothing wrong with that. I certainly took a long time finding myself. However, I positioned myself so when I did finally decide what I wanted to do, I would be prepared.

Education is the key to excelling, no matter what field you want to enter. Having an apprenticeship or internship, taking a continuing education class, or simply working with a mentor can set the stage for entering a career or owing your own business with something more than just dreams of success.

Now that I am embarking on a new journey of entrepreneurship, I have been exposed to different kinds of opportunities that I did not realize exist. You can't work toward a goal if you don't have one. The only way to make progress is to first acknowledge there is a problem.

Don't go through life waiting to be rescued. So many people are so focused on being rescued; they miss the fact that they can save themselves.

Being confident of this very thing, that He who has begun a good work in you will complete it until the day of Jesus Christ... Philippians 1:6

5

*For I know the plans
I have For You*

ime sure does fly; for it seems like it was just yesterday when I was rocking my baby boy in my arms. It's been 20 years and my baby is now a young man; he's almost outgrown me.

My son Nijirren was diagnosed with having a learning disability at the age of three as he displayed some developmental delays during his early years.

Talking and walking was a challenge for him and it wasn't until he began pre-k, is when he really started to talk and walk to a degree where he didn't need coaching.

He began school at the age of three and started receiving early intervention and speech therapy to accommodate his developmental delays.

His teachers would visit with him in the home to give him that extra support and therapy in addition to time spent at school in the classroom.

My mother had him so spoiled; dependent on the bottle and the nuk for a very long time. She was the one basically raising him in his early years because I was always working or in the streets partying doing what teenagers enjoyed doing. Or might I say doing what teenagers weren't supposed to be doing. Although I did some things and went some places I shouldn't have at that time, my son was always my number one priority.

I worked very hard to provide the things he needed in the absence of his father. My mother helped me out a lot too as well as my dad as I was still a child myself trying to navigate this thing called life.

He was the little boy my mother never had but always wanted, so she referred to him as her son. It didn't bother me one way or the other because I was just glad I had an around the clock baby sitter free of charge.

Nijirren was given an IEP all throughout elementary school because of his learning challenges. I frequently had to attend meetings at the school and be involved in shaping his education plan.

I didn't want him to feel like he was any different from any of the other kids so he was still always in a regular classroom setting.

For those who are not familiar with an IEP (Individual Education Plan), it was put in place to help the child who is struggling academically because of a disability or illness that limits the child ability to perform in a regular academic setting. Similar to 504 and resource classes. Nijirren and so many other kids like him desire to perform on the same level as their peers but their abilities are limited and it's a struggle from day to day.

It sometimes frustrates me to see him struggle because I know his desire to perform above average is there and I see it every day but it is indeed a challenge for him.

Reading and Spelling are areas of strength for him and I must add that he can fluently read and spell better than some adults I know and work with every day. I stress to him how important it is to be able to read and write and he acknowledges that. He reads well but just like any other child; I must stay on him about reading regularly.

He recently graduated from high school and the journey was not at all easy. His senior year was a challenge and after having to transfer schools after we were affected by the historic flood of South Louisiana, really set things back for him and on top of that transferring schools to another parish.

That final IEP before graduation was intense and we shed some tears after learning that he would not be graduating on time with his senior class because he fell short a couple of credits needed to graduate on time. What a blow to the head that was for the both of us when I know he had worked so hard. I had already ordered his graduation package which cost hundreds of dollars and he had attended all the senior festivities and everything. So yeah that news was devastating but that did not discourage us one bit.

He knew giving up was not an option and he would do whatever it takes no matter what to finish strong and make his exit. His entire summer was spent going to summer school but he made it and the greatest feeling is knowing he did not quit and endured to the end. He indeed received his high school diploma. He had been a mentee in the 100 Black Men of Metro Baton Rouge Mentoring program for several years and this was his senior year in the program. He had the opportunity to march in with his cap and gown on in the program's culminating ceremony they have at the end of the session each year. He was overjoyed and proud that he could make his entrance wearing his cap and gown representing his high school.

I'm saddened when I see the numbers of juveniles dropping out of high school and I'm easily reminded of how that was me. I thought once I became pregnant that I did not stand a chance but I had it all wrong. Failure is not final and delayed is not denied! Now that I'm a mother I realize that children need support and guidance and if it's not given freely at home, then they will surely get it elsewhere.

Parents must be involved always and know what their kids are involved in. It's not enough to just say oh I know what my child is doing at all times because if truth be told, children get into all kinds of things when they are not monitored properly.

With social media and online connections steady on the rise, it's so easy for our children to get caught up in all types of mess. My appeal is to the parents and guardians to always be that person your children can talk to about anything. When children are not valued at home, they then usually turn to outside influences that oftentimes cause them more harm than good.

Train up a child in the way he should go,
And when he is old he will not depart from it.
Proverbs 22:6

{Parish Inn}

My first night working at the parish prison was a brand-new experience for me. Of all the places to work in the jail, I was assigned to the lockdown lines. From the moment, I opened the doors and entered the corridors of the jail, the aroma of stinky feet and butt crack hit me smack dead in the face.

The smell was one I thought I'll never get used to but I can assure you, I was wrong. Rotating twelve-hour shifts is what my regular work schedule consisted of. The great thing about my schedule was that I had the privilege of having every other weekend off which is different from what I was used to working before.

We were required to only work half of the year so although the hours were long and tiresome, we still had a lot of days off. We had days when we would be on mandatory call out so we had to be available on those days if needed.

After two nights of working lockdown and having to deal with offenders who refused to shower and take care of their personal hygiene, I was assigned to work with the female offenders on the opposite side of the jail.

The female facility holds approximately two hundred women and most of the time it's packed to the capacity just like the male housing units.

This area of the jail is separated from the male dorms and living quarters and it's operated slightly different from the men.

The female facility has four lines, dormitory style with each line holding 46 offenders. Each line has three shower stalls, three toilets connected to a sink, and 23 bunk beds in the dorm area.

The dayroom separates the dorm with bars and has a 32-inch flat screen television mounted on the wall, two pay phone style phones that only have the capability to place outgoing collect calls, and several tables with seats attached surrounding the dayroom for daytime entertainment.

There are also two lockdown lines which hold five on each line. Lockdown has only a bed made of concrete with a flat plastic mattress on top of it with a toilet and sink in the cell with one shower stall and one phone attached to the wall.

Anywhere from five to twenty new female intakes are booked into the jail daily. I call it Parish Inn because the offenders are in and out so frequently as if they are checking in and out of a five-star hotel. We constantly see the same ones get out and are right back within the following week and sometimes the following day.

With a high recidivism rate, the parole program's success story is often the exception rather than the rule.

There are several programs at the jail offered to help and encourage the offenders to live a life that is free of crime. Such programs for example are Alcoholics Anonymous (AA), free indeed, and reality behind bars; just to name a few. Religious services are offered daily to those who wish to participate.

All offenders must be strip searched each time they are escorted from one location to another. The main reason for conducting a strip search is to prevent prisoners from smuggling contraband into the jail. Contraband is anything a prisoner is not allowed to have while in custody.

After working with the female offenders for eight months, I was ready for a change. I was offered a position in Central Booking and I didn't think twice about transferring out. I was ready to do something new.

Central Booking is the new intake processing and release department of the jail. I would consider this area to be the busiest and most chaotic in the entire jail because so much goes on in booking. I was up for the challenge that many others were not willing to take on.

The noise coming from the city and district court tanks was beginning to drive me crazy my first few days working in booking; so many different conversations at the same time with occasional outbursts of laughter from one side to another.

The air was stale with the smell of musk or some other awful undesirable odor that can come from 50 to 100 men gathered together in one big room. It's a smell you eventually grow accustomed to while being a deputy working in the inmates housing area.

Jail is a dangerous institution and every day I step foot into that place, my life was at risk. It's dangerous working in that type of environment but someone must do it. Despite all the crap we had to put up with working at this adult day care, I loved my job and the people associated with it.

As an officer of the law, I did my job well and I extend to the inmates all the opportunities they are entitled to while in my custody. Some deputies don't give a hoot and will call the inmates a scum bag to their face. I try to leave judgment up to the judge and the jury so I just maintain care, custody and control while on duty.

Some deputies will proudly tell the inmates not to ask them for shit, not even a roll of toilet paper. Those officers express their anger and disgust and it's passed from one shift to the next. I could never treat others any different than how I expect to be treated regardless of my position.

The murderers and the traffic violators, the sick and the well are all housed together so I don't know who did what unless they told me, so I treat all of them with the same respect.

To some inmates, jail offers better comforts than their home life: Three meals a day, a bed with clean linen, laundry service, color cable TV, and affordable medical care unlike the deteriorating neighborhoods where many of them come from. Some were lucky to get one meal a day, let alone three. Many are homeless so the extortion that happens is nothing in comparison to life on the streets in Baton Rouge.

In corrections, "time" is used as a form of punishment. Inmates serve a sentence which can range from days to months to years, or even life terms depending on the crime. As human beings, all we have in life is time and it's what we do with the time we have is what makes our lives meaningful.

I have few words for people who disrespect another person simply for personal pleasure. I know if I can make a difference in an inmate's life, I can do it better from the inside. It's sad to be on the inside and see so many men and women who don't have a clue about how to put their lives together. Some walk around jail like being incarcerated is a joke. Situations in jail can often change a person's life forever. You can't come and go as you please; the thing that freedom affords you.

In jail, you don't get the chance to eat the things you like; you can only have what is available, and very rarely is the food any good.

I share my stories to try to help others learn from my mistakes to avoid unnecessary pain. I know the Lord blesses me for my attempts, and I have no shame telling someone the struggle I went through to get where I am today.

All I can say is that God has had his hands on me and he has kept me safe in his arms. After experiencing and being involved in a total of four different automobile accidents and not sustaining any serious injuries from either of them, I'm convinced the Lord has me here for a reason because if not, death could have fell on me a long time ago but he knows the plans he has for me.

None of us are perfect but I can assure you that God knows your struggle and he hears your cry.

It's been five years now since I left the parish prison and since then went on to do other jobs in corrections. Working at the parish prison was a job like no other I had before and I'm thankful for the opportunity although I know some people would not be caught dead working in a prison.

It was a humbling experience and of all the jobs I've had over the years, I miss working there the most however I know God has called me to another area of corrections which is to advocate for the men and women who are locked away in the correctional system and forgotten about. Getting to see someone enter the unknown after having been in some unimaginable situations you've never been in before such as a murder or a rape and then walk into a place as humble as a bird after such a horrific act, makes you wonder long and hard about what go through the minds of people.

Who am I to judge when my sin is no different from the next man. Yes, my heart is saddened for those who are victims of crime and yes those who are responsible should pay the price for their actions. You do the crime so you do the time or whatever the price to pay may be.

My colleagues often joked and called me the social worker, the term we give to deputies and officers who empathize with the inmates. Despite my compassion for the lost, I was always firm but fair and I received much respect and that did not come easy for a lot of deputies I worked alongside of.

After 9 years of working in Corrections, God has now called me to a new assignment that involves advocating for Criminal Justice Reform. There is a national movement to reform the criminal justice system like never seen before and there has been a call to action to speak up and speak out for those locked behind prison walls with no voice.

Jails and the prison conditions across the country are deplorable and I have made it my mission to call these unjust practices out for what they are. Some of the unjust laws in Louisiana criminal code are overrated and need to be removed from the books. With my state of Louisiana holding the number one spot for many things that shine a negative light on us and especially when it comes to our incarceration rate and the unjust laws, I want to be part of the change.

I know we can do better but it's gone take people getting in the trenches putting in the work and encouraging others to come work alongside of us.

Trust in the Lord with all your heart,
And lean not on your own understanding; In all
your ways acknowledge Him,
And He shall direct your paths... Proverbs 3:5-6

{Too Much Drama for Me}

One fool after another! Where do they come from? My dating game was a capital H.O.T Mess! I will reflect on one of my past relationships that could have turned out deadly but God knows the plans he has for me and death wasn't in his divine plan.

My ex-boyfriend Rondale, who was a little younger than I was, became my lil boo thang while we were working together at the same restaurant some years ago. I normally didn't go out with guys younger than I was but after he harassed me continuously about talking to him, I finally gave him a chance.

Things started out great at first but it wasn't long before he started to show his true colors which began to be a problem. He was very jealous and anytime he saw me talking to other men, he would act a fool. I didn't know at that time that he was bi-polar but it wasn't long before I learned he had some issues. One minute he was sweet and loving and the next he would just go off the handle.

It was always drama with him. He had issues with his family, his job, his so-called friends; just too much drama for me. I found myself in a jacked-up situation and I constantly wondered how I was gonna get out this one because he was abusive mentally and physically and I knew it wouldn't be easy to break it off with Rondale.

We went at it toe to toe too many times for me to remember. He snatched my brand-new wig off my head one day when we were into it and what he did that for, I lit in on his behind. We really went at each other that day and afterwards there was peace for a while after that episode.

The drama kicked off again eventually. One particular incident was a wakeup call for me though. One evening we were arguing as I was getting ready for work. At some point, he decided he didn't want me to go to work because he'd rather me stay home with him for the evening so he wouldn't be alone.

That wasn't going to happen, well that is what I thought anyway. I was ready for work and about to head out the door but as soon as I proceeded to turn the knob to walk out the door, I suddenly felt something pressed tightly against my waist. He had gotten his revolver from the drawer and told me if I knew what was good for me, I wouldn't step foot out that door.

My heart skipped ten beats. I just stood there still in silence waiting for whatever was going to happen next. He demanded that I lie down in the bed with him and take a nice little nap. To the bed is where I quickly went escorted by him and that old rusty revolver. Shortly after we lay down in the bed, he was sound asleep with the gun still pressed at my side under the covers.

He was asleep and of course I was wide awake praying and asking God to spare my life. He answered my prayers again like I knew he would. I had the opportunity at this moment to take Rondale out of his misery had I been a killer.

But instead of me using that same weapon he used to assault me with, I quietly and carefully got out of bed and I removed the gun from his hands. I felt sorrier for him more than anything. I knew he needed help. I didn't even involve the police because as much pain he had put me through, I still didn't want to see him go to jail.

Amazingly, I felt as if my life had great value and it wasn't the end for me. I was terrified of guns but a sense of assurance came over me that made me know God was present and everything was all good. Needless to say, I believe I handled the situation differently from a person who had not been saved and led by the spirit.

I know you're probably thinking by now, oh she's crazy just like him. But no, I'm far from it. Yes, I should have had him arrested or you may be thinking, I should have blown out his marbles for playing with me when I had the chance but that wasn't what I thought was best for me to do at that time.

I had much sympathy for him because he had shared with me countless of horrifying stories of how he witnessed his father abuse his mother. He needed help and he was hurting inside because he still held on to all those painful memories.

Unfortunately, I wasn't the one who was successful in reaching him but I put forth much effort. He is history in my book now. Too much drama for me!

I know there are many people who have been in an abusive relationship and some are still going through it. I've heard women say that if he doesn't rough me up a little then he doesn't care about me.

Where in the world you come up with a lie like that. It's insane! I'm here to tell you that abuse and love don't fit into the same category.

I knew this wasn't the way it was supposed to be because I wasn't exposed to abuse in my home growing up as a child and I'm very blessed to have been raised in a loving home where abuse wasn't the norm. Love is kind, love is patient, love does not abuse.

Love is taking action, not a feeling and it took me some time to learn that. I've had my share of heartache and pain from investing my time and energy in people who didn't mean me any good. I've learned that you teach people how to treat you and if someone is treating you anything less of respect and honor then you have created and allowed that toxic relationship to form.

Love does not hurt. If someone is making you hurt, then they do not love you. It has been a long time coming for me but today I'm stronger and I'm wiser. I don't allow people into my circle who don't bring any value and I don't want to be in your circle if I can't bring value to you.

If you are the one always giving and never receiving, then it may be time to part ways with that relationship.

All that drama was over ten years ago and since then I've met a wonderful man I can now call my husband. I had my doubts about marrying again but I can assure you now that marriage can be beautiful if we make it our mission to make the best of it. We aren't the perfect couple but I can say that we are learning and growing together each day by the Grace of God and it gets sweeter with every passing moment.

God is our refuge and strength, A very present help in trouble. Therefore, we will not fear, Even though the earth be removed, And though the mountains be carried into the midst of the sea; Though its waters roar and be troubled, Though the mountains shake with its swelling... Selah Psalm 46:1-3

6

I Can Do Nothing on My Own

*A*s a believer in Christ, I am called to live a more simple life. The problem with a complex life, one that demands so many conveniences and gadgets, is that it requires too much money and too many resources. There is never enough to get everything we want or think we need. I find there is always something else I want.

It may be another item for the house, a new dress, or another bottle of fragrance. I have had to struggle prayerfully, to establish priorities for my needs and wants. There are times when I think I must have something, but if I will wait a few days, I find I can live without it.

I believe that any person who knows and loves God must deal with the question "what does it mean to follow him"? I believe an honest evaluation will lead to the conclusion that as followers of Christ, we must be something other than a reflection of our culture.

All the things we have received from the hands of a gracious and loving father are to be shared— and in many instances—given away completely. As

I have tried to incorporate this truth into my life and style of living, the Lord has called on me to share my possessions in all kinds of ways.

Trying to live a simpler life is not easy. I struggle with it every day as I try to establish priorities in my life. I carefully consider things like what books to read, how to use my time, which new responsibilities of service to take on, or even how to rest and relax.

There will be tension in trying to live a balanced life and trying to stay focused on the only one who can give us the proper perspective.

It is the responsibility of each person to examine his or her own personal life and look for ways to structure simplicity into it. Perhaps the first thing that must happen is the realization of a need for change. After that, the needed courage and grace must be sought from the Lord.

I must ask God constantly to help me achieve my top priority of living differently. I must set aside a time for quietness and meditation. This means some chores are left undone, but I am usually able to finish the most essential ones. Changing a life takes a lot of redirecting of the will and practice at discipline.

As a young woman, I have had to accept his call just like anybody else. Having been poverty-stricken for many years is no excuse. God has used some of those injuries to help me become more sensitive and more concerned about the poverty of others.

There is nothing glamorous about poverty, but it can serve as a creative force in one's life. Living from paycheck to paycheck is not a lifestyle that is pleasing but I thank God, every day for the jobs I have had. I've learned to be content with what God has already blessed me with instead of focusing on what I think I should have.

Perhaps it is harder for poor people or black people to live a life of simplicity but he never calls us to do anything without giving us the grace to do it. If he brought you to it then he sure will bring you through it is my philosophy. I can do nothing on my own without him leading the way.

Way too many people are stressed out these days over things we have no control over. More and more people are taking medication for high blood pressure and sales are up on energy boosters. Work overload is having a negative impact on people and it's just devastating to see so many who can't seem to get their lives in order.

I make it a point not to overwork myself although I can definitely use the extra money but it's just not worth it.

Yes, we have been called to a new way of living. The joyous truth is that God stands ready to give us all the gifts we need to make the journey.

{For who hopes for what he sees?}

Okay so we all make mistakes. We all have our share of failures in life. Lord knows I've had mine. But mistakes, even a series of them, do not necessarily mean the end of the world and most important; do not give you the license to wallow in perpetual dysfunction.

We all make decisions that we wish we could take back. Sometimes these choices have a profoundly negative impact and make our lives more difficult. But you can't allow regret and bitterness to extinguish your hopes and dreams of a better life for yourself and your children.

Everyone's job is shaky, money is funny, credit is bad, pressure is high—everyone has their own problems. We can't allow our present circumstances to dictate our potential in this world. There are many resources available to help rebuild our lives but we are so busy concentrating on what we cannot do, what we don't have and how bad things are for us, and what others have that we can't see the world of opportunities awaiting anyone who wishes to go out and get it.

For the last two decades, we've measured success in bling and things. Our relentless pursuit of stuff has often been stronger than our pursuit of education, healthy families and strong communities.

Our image of success has changed. Somewhere between the Cosby show and the real housewives of Atlanta, we lost our way. Success is not having the fancy clothes and the cars and taking lavish trips every week but success to me is being the best I can be at whatever I put my hands to.

It doesn't matter what God has called me to, I will do it with grace and excellence. Success is a journey and we never really reach a destination with success because I believe God continues to call us to different assignments throughout our lives.

There are no excuses. It is time for us to realize we have the potential to turn our condition around even if we've done a poor job at managing our lives thus far. If you can have Facebook friends in fifteen different countries and follow your favorite celebrities on Instagram, then you can find out anything you need to know.

Unlike so many people in nations around the world, we can change our circumstances. We can stop, reflect and decide to change the direction of our lives at any time. So, your life is a mess; instead of using all your energy to figure out why it's someone else fault, figure out how you can use the resources provided by your community or family and friends to turn things around. Show your children that every setback is not a disaster, that they have power to change the game with dedication and a little hustle.

Too many men have children all over town and don't support any of them. Children need their fathers to be there to read to them and play games with them. And they need them to listen to them and teach them how to be young men and women. They don't need your $75.00 a week as much as they need you to be there when they win their first science fair award. Support isn't just the money the government takes out of your check and forces you to pay.

I'm not exempt from this epidemic because my son has not spoken to or seen his father in a very long time. My son receives no type of support emotionally or financially from his father and it has been that way for a while. My son has learned to deal with his father's absence although I know he would love to have that relationship again he once experienced with his dad many years ago.

And although many women complain about their children's fathers not being in their lives, I am here to say that there is a huge problem with women keeping their children away from their dads and using them as pawns in petty games.

I have never used my son as a way to get back at his father. Of course, it's a shame if a man doesn't provide support for his children financially but financial support isn't a way to buy time with them. To withhold a child from his/her father because of your own spite, anger, and money issues or bitterness is just wrong and only punishing the child who deserves all the love he or she can get.

It is only by the grace of God that I have come this far. It is true that I have been in situations that could have easily derailed my life. It is true that I have been irresponsible, selfish and reckless. Does that exempt me from challenging others to do better than I did?

I've learned from my mistakes and although some of the things I've done could have easily taken me out, I never lost sight of my goals. There was a strange disconnect between my real life and my play life. As bad as I was, I was good when it counted.

I want the best for everyone. I want everybody to win. There is enough out here for everyone, I don't compete. I strive for excellence and don't make excuses anymore. I am very aware of my shortcomings and I constantly strive to improve.

When I say we must do the best we can with what we have, it means that excellence isn't about money. It's about embracing life and striving for achievement and competence. It's about showing up even when we don't have all the answers. People are waiting on us to show up. Our children are depending on us to lead the way.

No government program can give you the desire to improve your life. No social worker can tell you how to dream big and have a vision beyond your current reality. We all have a role to play in being the best we can be. We need to make better decisions about parenthood & relationships, finances & work, and education & spirituality. Period. The problem is, if we are all acting like we're twenty-one, who will become the next leaders in the community?

Who do young people look to as examples of how to behave when the grown-ups are bending over and touching their toes in the club right next to them?

Social media has just made it so easy to put our foolishness on display for the world to see. Social media can be a positive tool and it can also be a nightmare all at the same time. What is posted on social media can be a blessing for some but a curse to others. It all depends on who receives the message and how it is received.

Social media I believe is a great tool and I try to make good use of it to share positive stories and stories that give hope. The message I want my followers to receive when they see me post on social media is that I love people, I love my family, I love God and I work hard for everything I've ever accomplished. That's it. I'm not out here trying to sell anyone a dream. It is what it is!

I also realize that not everyone will receive my message in the way I intend for it to be received and that is okay. Some people choose to dwell on the negative and some just will not see you for who you really are at the core. Some will focus on who you used to be and where you used to go and what you used to do. Don't focus on those naysayers because I have learned that some people are just annoyed by your anointing. They can't stand to see you blessed. They don't understand the favor on your life. You my friend choose peace. The peace of God that surpasses all understanding. And when you choose peace, you no longer must try to figure out why people treat you the way they do or why people hate on you for no reason. You will learn that it was all necessary. It's painful but it's necessary to take you to the next level.

Fear not, for I am with you; be not dismayed, for I am your God. I will strengthen you, yes, I will help you, I will uphold you with My righteous right hand... Isaiah 14:10

7

She is More

Profitable than Silver

*W*hat is more devastating than going through life feeling you have no worth? Being beautiful is a state of mind. It has nothing to do with your physical self. You never know what you are capable of until you decide what you want and then you just have to go for it. You can do anything that you put your mind to. It starts in the mind.

{Salt of the Earth}

Summer was coming to an end and a new season in my life was about to begin. We all make those plans in our mind to turn over a new leaf for the New Year. Although the New Year was still months away, I had already started making plans in advance. With graduation six months away, I knew it was time to start making some changes.

I wanted to believe I was saved but deep down I knew I wasn't living a life that was pleasing to God. My faith in God wasn't strong enough to stand against the temptations and deceit of the enemy. In my mind, I thought everything was all good between me and God as long as I was studying the word here and there and going to church on Sunday morning. But eventually I came to realize that was not enough and God needed more from me; I needed more from me.

The day was that of September 15th, 2009 and the congregation was fired up at New Gideon as usual. Voices of Gideon were singing my favorite hymns and I was delighted to be in the house of the Lord one more time. I couldn't sit still in my seat; fired up for Jesus is how I describe my excitement and stimulation.

After all the extras that we do from the program on a Sunday morning; the welcome, the mission statement, acknowledgements and announcements, tithes and offering, etc.; you know how we Baptist folk get down, there was a word from the Lord. Pastor always know how to keep us rejoicing on Sunday morning. The only thing running through my mind the entire 45 minutes the sermon was being delivered was I needed to desperately make a move when the doors to the church open. The moment of the service we refer to as the alter call. It takes place immediately after the preacher finishes delivering his message.

The moment of truth had finally come. After Pastor had spoken the words "If there's anybody here who needs to dedicate or rededicate their life to the Lord, you can come" Surprisingly, I was the first one up and out into the isle of the church. I grabbed my son by the hand and within seconds, we were standing at the alter facing the congregation.

This was the moment I had contemplated for so long and there I was with tears pouring down my face staring at a crowd full of hurting people. I sensed that there were many others out in the crowd wishing they had the faith and courage to make a move for God. Come One, Come All, lyrics was flowing from my mouth. It wasn't long before I was surrounded by people who desired to give their lives to the Lord.

I expressed my desire to be baptized and become a member of the body of Christ. My pastor assured me that New Gideon was not a perfect church but where we lacked in perfection, we make up in love. I had witnessed him express his love for the Lord to new members time and time again

I began my fellowship at New Gideon Baptist Church (NGBC) in Baton Rouge, Louisiana eight months prior to this date after I was invited by my sister who had been attending frequently after she was invited by a friend and member of the church. After earnestly praying and asking God to place me in a loving and Bible teaching church home, he led me to New Gideon. I was now one week away from baptism; an experience I had never experienced before at the age of twenty-seven years and nine months young.

The entire week following my life changing experience, I was so excited and I told everyone I was going to be baptized. I attended a new members class held immediately after service that prepared new believers in Christ for rebirth and following the ways of God. The class taught me what it means to be baptized and what I can expect following this special occasion.

Now I was anticipating the Holy Spirit to come over me and I was expecting to feel a different feeling inside. I had read in the Bible where Jesus said, "you shall be baptized with the Holy Spirit". I had this belief that I would be a totally different person when I came out of the water. Well that is what I desired anyway. I wanted to be changed with no work involved. I expected the water to change me; my way of thinking, and my behavior; my entire attitude.

If only I knew then what I know now, I probably would have been spared from some of the heartache and pain I experienced as a teenager and young adult. I'm a firm believer that faith without works is as dead as a stiff body on the front pew on a Sunday morning.

The day had finally come and I had spent all week preparing for me and Nijirren's baptism. My son also accepted Jesus as his Lord and savior on this day. He was just as excited as I was and he was eleven at the time. He didn't quite understand everything but he acknowledged this was a moment of great significance in both of our lives.

I was dressed in all white because white is a color of purity and this day I felt pure and cleansed. I was about to lay it all at the altar and have my sins washed away. God said he would forgive me and no longer remember my sins so I was ready for this new life God had promised.

Immediately following the final announcements at the end of the service, Pastor announced he had two to be baptized and instructed everyone to remain seated and witness the ceremony. After the elders and deaconess finished prepping me and loving on me in the dressing area, I strutted a few steps down to the lake of new beginnings. Pastor and one of the deacons held my hand and led me to the baptismal pool located directly behind the choir stand. The words, I baptize you in the name of the Father, the Son, and the Holy Spirit had never sounded so convincing than now.

After I was baptized, I began to seek out ways to become actively involved in ministry. My love and compassion for people was a constant reminder that I needed to help make a difference in the church and in the world.

The concept of seed time and harvest wasn't something I could generally identify with because I wasn't raised in the country on a farm but I understood the concept of "you reap what you sow". Many believers' understanding of planting and sowing seeds has only to do with finances. This misconception has hindered a lot of people from doing effective work in the ministry because we think if we're not giving money, we can be used in ministry.

Everywhere we go and everything we do, we leave behind seeds which we plant whether it is good seeds or bad seeds. It's up to us whether we choose to bear good fruit or bad fruit.

God expects each of us to bless others with our gifts and this is not just limited to money. It's good to bless others with money and resources, but sharing our talents is far more important than a dollar bill.

When I look at the world around me and reflect on the fact that there are people hurting and seeking relief, I'm constantly reminded of the children of Israel. I see our people perishing from a lack of knowledge while the enemy is doing a happy dance. Crime is at an all-time high and instead of coming together with solutions to our problems; many just want to blame the devil for the condition we're in. The devil gets way too much credit and God gets too little glory.

The purpose for me writing this book is to minister to those in need of healing. Let me put it to you straight "You can heal your life", despite your situation. My ultimate desire is that this book land in the hands of someone who will be touched and moved by my struggles yet encouraged by my victories.

Every chance I get, I search for opportunities to meet others right where they are. I know what it feels like when you think you're all alone in this world by yourself. I've been there! I've been mistreated, used, abused and misunderstood by many but that is not where my story end.

Some of the choices I've made could have very well taken me out but God has a plan for me. And the greatest news of all time is that He has a plan for each one of us. So, what if your life is a mess! There is absolutely nothing that is too difficult for God to handle. Your trials will eventually turn into your testimony even if you can't see past your current situation right now.

If you're reading this book and you're at a season in your life where everything is all good and God is working in your favor; great! I encourage you to be a blessing and inspiration to someone else. Just be mindful, there will come a time when you will be taken away from your comfort zone; just keep living. Faith in God is all you will have to stand on!

For this very reason, we should rejoice when things are going good and when things are not so good. We need a faith that expresses to God, that when we are down to our very last, we will still praise him and give him the glory he deserves. We were made in his image and it all goes right back to him.

So many of us have allowed fear and pride to hinder us from the work of ministry. Fear of not having all the answers. God has not given us a spirit of fear; fear is a rotten fruit directly from the enemy. Satan doesn't want us to minister to others because ministry equips us with the power and knowledge to defeat his army.

No need to keep searching for a key to an unlocked door. The kingdom is already within us. All we need to do is tap into it. Stop waiting for God to bless something you have not presented to him. If you have not put that thing out front and center, how do you expect God to bless it my friend. Faith without works is DEAD!

It's been nine years now since I gave my back life to the Lord and became a member of the New Gideon Baptist Church in Baton Rouge, Louisiana. Nine years ago, I didn't know where this journey would lead me but I can say it has been one full of tests yet magnified with triumphs. Today I serve in several different areas of ministry with my teaching and ministering to the youth being my proudest charge from God. As a Sunday school teacher for the teens, I'm always reminded of how lost I was at their age.

We as parents and educators need to educate and empower our children. I don't just teach them about God and the bible but I teach practical life lessons as well because our children are depending on us. Show them and teach them what nobody ever told them.

There are so many distractions and things that can easily keep our children's attention that does not promise anything good. We must show up for our kids and not only in the church but outside the church too. Volunteer out in the community. There are many volunteer opportunities where we can help make a difference in the life of our children.

Serving as Usher and Deaconess for several years has also taught me so much about people and life. I would not trade my experiences for anything and it has been an honor to serve God's people in this capacity. My family who I love dearly supports me and my children are active in youth ministry. To God be all the Glory for where this journey has taken me.

We all have a story and experiences that has helped us to become who we are. I don't think I regret going through anything I have went through because without those life lessons I don't know how things would have unfolded for me.

I do know we must be intentional in our actions and what we say and do. I have not always been intentional. I must be intentional with having a consistent prayer life and study period with God. I can't pour into others what I don't have. The more God pours in to me I can give to others.

I must be intentional about fasting and abstaining from certain foods and things that are a distraction. I know this is a struggle for many people especially in the world we live in where there is an abundance of everything. So many choices without limit.

We indeed serve an unlimited God but there comes a time when we must put limits on what we do and how we behave. We can't just live any kind of way if we are called to be examples. People are searching for a sprinkle of hope and encouragement and you just may be the only hope they see.

Do not conform and do not compromise what you believe in just to be liked or accepted by others. Don't sell yourself short on social media just to get a bunch of likes or comments. Take time to learn who you are in Christ. Don't expect people to follow you when you don't have a clue who you are. Trust and believe the followers will come authentically when they sense you know who you are and that you are real.

You are called to a standard of excellence. Not a standard of perfection but you should be operating in the greatness God has called you to.

God specializes in the sick and is married to the sinner. He meets us right where we are! If we could save ourselves then we wouldn't need a savior at all. Our father already knows everything about us and he wants to help us but we must submit to the spirit. It's up to us! He knows we are full of sin and unworthy of his grace and mercy but he still embraces us anyway. That is what I love about him! While we were still sinners, he sent his Son to die for us.

It is what it is! This isn't something I heard, it's what I know. So now, instead of spending my Thursday evenings at happy hour throwing back 2 for 1 shots after I get off work, I'm delighted to spend my time at mid-week service praying and receiving a word from the Lord. My dancing and shouting in the church house is more fun than I could have ever had in the club getting drunk and waking up with a terrible hangover.

Charm is deceptive, and beauty is fleeting; but a woman who fears the LORD is to be praised.
Proverbs 31:30

8

When You Have a Vision

he bible tells us in Proverbs 29:18, Where there is no vision, the people perish. Vision is defined as the ability to see: sight or eyesight; something that you imagine: a picture that you see in your mind; something that you see or dream especially as part of a religious or supernatural experience.

In Biblical times God sent visions to people as prophesies. Let me first say that God has a vision for what we are to be doing with our time here. God's vison for you is what you were made for.

You see I didn't always have a vision for my life and although I could see physically, I was still spiritually blind to the things and ways of God. When I think of vision I'm always reminded of a former coworker who was physically blind yet he had so much wisdom.

I clearly remember a conversation we had right before he retired. He had just recently returned to work after being out for several months due to the historic flood we experienced here in South Louisiana. When I got word, he was back at work I made it a point to go over and speak and let him know I was happy to see him back.

We talked for quite some time and he told me how grateful he was to still be alive after his experience with the flood.

I was also affected by the historic flood and had to leave my home and live in a hotel for several months so we had something in common to talk about. He and his wife who is also blind too was displaced from their home for a while following the flood. We had talked briefly before in the past and made small talk from time to time but the conversation we had this time was different and after talking with him, I began to think about vision and sight in a totally different light.

This conversation was not too long ago so the details are still fresh in my mind.

What made me hold on to the details of this conversation was the joy I experienced from seeing his joy as he talked to me about the goodness of God. He spoke with joy in his heart as he told me about losing almost everything he owned in the flood. He told me of near death situations in his past and how God had changed his life.

Despite his physical blindness he had a vision and he had a vision that some people have yet to experience. This is a man who could not see in the natural but it was evident he had vision. He eventually received everything back that was destroyed in the flood.

He told me he now has things that he did not have before and that he stayed faithful and true to the one who would get him through. This conversation I had with this former coworker is just one of many where I was left inspired and more eager to act on the vision I believe God gave me.

Obtaining vision is something far more important than having good eyesight. Helen Keller was once asked, "What would be worse than being born blind?" to which she replied, "Having sight without a vision." My God!

In the case of your divinely ordered vision, God goes to work in you to prepare you for what he knows lies ahead. Your vision is simply an extension of his vision. And his timing is perfect.

Twenty years ago, when I became pregnant with my son at 15 and dropped out of high school, I could not see past my current situation. I could not see myself returning to school and one day graduating college. I could not see myself living for God and serving in ministry. I could not see myself walking in victory and living on purpose. As I mentioned earlier, Proverbs 29:18 started to resonate with me after I began to see clearly. Although I could see in the natural, in the spiritual I had a lack of vision and guess what, I was perishing because of it.

The place where I am now today, I believe God had already helped prepare me to be here right now in this season for this reason. We sometimes have visions and dreams inside of us but we don't always know if God gave them to us or not.

God's ultimate plan for your life reaches beyond the visions he's given you for your family, business, ministry, and finances. Above and beyond the achievements associated with your vision, God wants to draw people to himself. Our visions are means to a greater end, namely the glory of God and the salvation of men and women. This is his ultimate objective, his ultimate desire.

When I was given a vision that I was supposed to be helping others, God began to place me in situations where I was given the opportunity to help and serve others. As I mentioned earlier, I have been serving as an usher in the church for several years now and when I was first given this vision I was to serve my church, I was not sure in what capacity I would serve but I could see it in my mind.

Even on my jobs, I started to see how I was impacting others just by being present and showing up. I once heard a preacher say in a bible study one time, that your job is blessed because you are there. You are the one who is holding the job together and bringing peace when the environment is not so pleasant at times.

God uses us in ways sometimes we can't even understand. Your life has power! After leaving not one, not two but three different jobs and seeing how my departure impacted people to the point they were literally in tears after learning I was leaving, I could not brush that off as a mere coincidence. This type of influence is not to be taken lightly and I always want to bring value in everything I do. How are you making a difference in the lives of others? What type of legacy are you building for your family and others who follow you?

Anything that we wish to manifest in our lives, we must first see it in our mind. It all starts in the mind. I'm sure you have heard the saying as a man thinketh so is he which comes directly from our bible.

So, I began to see myself serving in the church and suddenly before I knew it I was doing just what I was seeing in my mind. Having vision means being able to visualize. Visualizing is the beginning of fulfilled vision. A man or woman of vision fully believes the impossible dream is possible.

Perhaps the most powerful aspect of vision is that it changes your way of thinking, which in turn changes the way you live. Vision is a power that motivates us to do great things, give great things, and love always.

Vision keeps us going when there doesn't appear to be any other reason to keep pushing forward toward the goal. It is so important to have the proper vision for our lives because worldly things like money, fame, fortune, influence, recognition, and worldly excellence don't satisfy the soul. Here is what King Solomon had to say about his self-centered vision in Ecclesiastes 2:11: "Yet when I surveyed all that my hands had done and what I had toiled to achieve, everything was meaningless, a chasing after the wind; nothing was gained under the sun."

From Solomon's writings, we conclude that any personal vision apart from God's will for our lives is incomplete. Despite the magnitude of our personal accomplishments; there will always be some void when we do it without God's blessing. Only when we work with God, and co-create with God will we be complete, joyful, and energetic people.

That's why we see so much discontent in the world; because people are not working together with a common vision of serving God. A worldly, self-centered vision is not the type of vision our Lord hoped that we would embrace. Knowing God's vision for His people means that we respond with a personal vision for our lives that is consistent with God's plan.

For many people, this is something that is very difficult. How do we know what is God plan for our lives? Most of us don't even know what our own vision is all about; so how do we find about God's vision for our lives.

We need to first communicate with God and learn to better love Him, trust Him, and live entirely for His glory. This means that we must start with a daily prayer. When we pray to God, we should do it in such a way that we thank Him for His blessings that we ask forgiveness from our sins, that we communicate our needs, and let Him know that our entire lives are open to serve Him.

Having vision does not mean that we develop a plan for our lives; but rather that we have a journey mapped out where we are in a constant state of movement. Having vision also means that we are actively working towards implementing God's vision for our lives.

When I was given a vision to write this book, I did not have all the specifics but I did know I could see the works of my fingers and what I believe in my heart would help many women and some men. I knew that women and men needed to be inspired and motivated to do what I believe God has called us to do.

I see so many people stuck and not embracing opportunities that I know would change their lives for the better. It took me ten years before I decided to go back to school and earn my high school diploma.

Before I took that leap of faith because God knows my academic skills were a little rusty after being out of school for so many years after dropping out in the 11th grade, I had to see myself as a student again first.

When I started to see myself working hard and studying, making good grades and one-day walking across the stage to receive my diploma, that is when I began to believe I knew I could do this and that I needed to do this. And now ten years later after receiving my GED, I'm two classes away from earning my Master's degree. Yes, you heard me right! I'll be holding my Master's degree in Public

Administration in a few short weeks. All this manifested because I had a vision and God was part of that vision so I knew I could not and would not fail.

Although I had this vision, that does not mean everything was all laid out for me and everything was clear. I had the vision but I was not sure how I would get to the promise.

Everything our hearts desire, God has already promised it to us, we just have to receive it. We may experience a few bumps in the road before making it to our promise but this is mainly due to our own stubbornness and disobedience oftentimes.

Always be prepared for whatever opportunities that may come your way. Educate yourself continuously. You should always be learning and growing and it doesn't have to be in a traditional setting where you are at school in a classroom. There are all types of free resources and training courses you can learn new skills.

Get out and volunteer in your community. There are always volunteer opportunities you can take advantage of. Giving back to my community is so important to me. Volunteering teaches you new skills and helps you discover strengths you didn't know you had.

One volunteer opportunity I had was a phone crisis intervention specialist. When I tell you, I didn't know I had it in me to help prevent someone from ending their life.

I knew this assignment would be whew a challenge and I figured that out from the training before we were ever released to take real calls from real people in a crisis. The training was very intense but of course we would be dealing with real people with real problems so we had to prepared.

Imagine having to listen to other people stories of misguided hope and helplessness at a time of crisis such as the historic flood we experienced here in South Louisiana when you are going through the same thing they are going through. Although I was living in a hotel because of the loss I experienced due to the flood, I still showed up for those in need. I still had hope and I still had my life and a lot of people did not have that after this tragic experience.

So, it was a humbling experience and I'm grateful for the skills I learned. It has helped me to be more compassionate of others. I was always a person who had compassion for others but after serving as a crisis intervention specialist, it really opened my eyes to how much mental illness, depression, and hopelessness is all around us

One thing I've done in all my previous jobs that offered free trainings and classes, I took advantage and I have all types of certificates for voluntarily taking advantage of those opportunities. Oftentimes I would be the only person from my department to attend the classes but I knew it would help me in leadership roles in the future. Every day I'm listening to something educational whether it is a YouTube video/tutorial or a Facebook live or a podcast while I'm driving in the car.

A traditional education such as college courses are expensive. I know from experience and have the student loan debt to show for it however we have so much free information and knowledge right at our fingertips.

I probably take more free online courses voluntarily because it's so much free information out there. Some of the free stuff is more useful than the courses I'm taking in college that is costing me thousands of dollars in tuition. All I'm saying is time out for the excuses. There is no way in the 21st century we should be perishing from a lack of knowledge when information is all around us.

I will end with this. When God gives you a vision, don't pretend you can't see it. We all have purpose and oftentimes our purpose is discovered through our dreams and visions. You are not here to just occupy a space until God calls you home. You were created to be queens and kings. Queens and Kings rule and they lead. You my sister are a queen! You my brother are a King! What are you going to do with the gift God has given you?

And it shall come to pass afterward, [that] I will pour out my spirit upon all flesh; and your sons and your daughters shall prophesy, your old men shall dream dreams, your young men shall see visions... Joel 2:28

In Loving Memory

Sandra (Sandy) Marie Sept-Gordon

January 17, 1951-February 24, 2007

My Mother My Angel

*F*IRST thanking God who gave me the vision and the zeal to write my first book. Thank you to my wonderful husband Andre, it's such a joy to have you in my life. Your continued love & support has helped me to branch out into new territory that I had never imagined before. My children-My Loves; Nijirren, Andrea & Andre Jr., you bring me so much joy... To all my family & friends close and extended, thank you for your support! And lastly, to all of you who have supported me through my business and ministry efforts, the relationships formed through social media near and far, I'm truly grateful.

~ Love You Much

Made in the USA
Columbia, SC
03 July 2022